# 101 ACTIVITIES FOR EXCEPTIONAL CHILDREN

by

**Edward R. Greaves**

*Cajon Valley Union School District*
*El Cajon, California*

**Lee P. Anderson**

*Vista Unified School District*
*Vista, California*

Peek Publications • P.O. Box 50123 • Palo Alto, California 94303

ISBN 0-917962-75-3

Library of Congress Catalog Card Number 81-85264

Manufactured in the United States of America

# Preface

*101 Activities* is a pocketful of motivational games and activities for all teachers—including physical education and classroom teachers—who are unfamiliar with "where to start" and "what to do." This resource for exceptional children is also designed to enhance and support existing physical education programs. It is especially valuable in regular classrooms with mainstreamed students—as many of the games have been specially developed to include the mainstreamed student. The book is divided into five sections: Motor Skills, Physical Fitness, Body Awareness, Social Behavior and Recreational Activities. The activities are in developmental order of difficulty within each section. Written in simple-to-follow directions, most utilize little or no equipment. Teaching hints are included on each activity for teaching the game or modifying the activity.

These "101 Activities for Exceptional Children" have been developed to: be success oriented, emphasize coordination and motor skills, promote positive self image and appropriate sports (group or social) conduct, and include all aspects of the "whole" child.

# Acknowledgments

We would like to express our sincere appreciation to several individuals who were instrumental in the writing (production) of *101 Activities for Exceptional Children.*

To Mrs. Jean M. Chappell for her careful editing of the manuscript and for numerous other tasks facilitating its production. To Mrs. Ginger Greaves and Mr. Red Stodghill for their many hours of typing and retyping. To Mr. Dwight Vallely for his above and beyond efforts with the photography.

Lee P. Anderson
Edward R. Greaves

# Table of Contents

# Equipment List

| Item | Quantity/Description | Item | Quantity/Description |
|------|---------------------|------|---------------------|
| Air Mattress | One | Bowling Pins | Ten |
| Balloons | Four dozen, 6'', 12'', 16'' | Bubble Mixture | Four ozs. |
| Backboard | One (basketball) | Buttons | Three dozen, ¾'' |
| Balls | | Cans (tennis ball containers) | Six |
|   Basketball | One | Carpet Squares | Twenty-one, 12'' x 24'' |
|   Beach Ball | Two | Cartons (ice cream) | Six, 12'' diameter |
|   Bowling Ball | Two | Chalk | One small box |
|   Cageball | One, small or large | Cones | Twelve, 12'' high (traffic cones) |
|   Football (Nerf) | Three | Crayons | Three boxes, elem. drawing |
|   Golfball | Two dozen, plastic | Finger Pops | Two dozen |
|   Nerf Balls | One dozen, 4'' and 8'' | Frisbee | One dozen, standard size |
|   Ping-Pong Balls | Two dozen | Frisbee (Nerf) | Six |
|   Playground Balls | Two 6'' balls, two 24'' balls | Handkerchief (rag) | One dozen, 12'' square |
|   Racquetballs | One dozen | Hockey Sticks | Six |
|   Soccer Ball | One | Net (volleyball) | One |
|   Softballs | Two | Newspapers | Six-inch thick newspaper |
|   Tennis Balls | One dozen | Paper | Twenty-five ft. (butcher) |
|   Tetherball | One, nylon cord attached | Parachute | One, 16 ft. diameter |
|   Volleyball | One | Pitchback | Two |
|   Wiffleball | Six, 4'' diameter | Pool | Three ft. dia. (plastic wading) |
|   Yarnball | One dozen, 4'' diameter | Scooter Boards | Twelve |
| Barrell | Three, 30 gal. plastic | Shuffleboard Set | One |
| Bases | Four, standard size | Shuffleball Table | See Activity for size |
| Bat | Two, plastic | Soap | One bar |
| Bean Bags | Three dozen, 4'' square | Stopwatches | Two |
| Blocks | One set, standard elem. bldg. | Sponges | One dozen, 2'' square |
| Bottles | Six, one-gallon size, plastic | Tape (masking) | One roll |
| Bowling Ramp | Two, roll-a-ball type | Tape Measure | One, 100 ft. long |
| | | Whistle | One |

# Activity Emphasis Chart

| Number | Activity | xx - Primary Emphasis<br>x - Secondary Emphasis | Page | Motor Skills | Physical Fitness | Body Awareness | Social Behavior | Recreation |
|---|---|---|---|---|---|---|---|---|
| 67 | Air Mattress Activity | | 75 | X | | XX | X | |
| 54 | Alligator Tag | | 59 | X | XX | | X | |
| 59 | Alphabet Switch | | 64 | | XX | | | |
| 34 | Back Away | | 36 | XX | | | | |
| 23 | Bag-It | | 25 | XX | XX | | | |
| 22 | Balloonics | | 24 | XX | | | | |
| 40 | Balloon Slap | | 45 | X | XX | | | |
| 50 | Balloon Volleyball | | 55 | | XX | | X | X |
| 11 | Barrel Hockey | | 13 | XX | | | | |
| 98 | Basket Barrel | | 112 | X | XX | | | |
| 60 | Basketball High Point | | 65 | X | XX | | | |
| 53 | Bean Bag Bandit | | 58 | | XX | | X | |
| 12 | Bean Bag Barrels | | 14 | XX | | | | |
| 8 | Big Five | | 10 | XX | | | | |
| 14 | Block Down | | 16 | XX | | | | |
| 51 | Blow Ball | | 56 | | XX | X | | |
| 45 | Blow Stations #1 - Bottle Blow | | 50 | | XX | | | |
| 46 | Blow Stations #2 - Blow Hockey | | 51 | | XX | | X | |
| 47 | Blow Stations #3 - Blow Track | | 52 | | XX | | X | |
| 48 | Blow Stations #4 - Big Blow | | 53 | | XX | | X | |
| 49 | Blow Stations #5 - Blow Relay | | 54 | | XX | | X | |
| 24 | Board Ball | | 26 | XX | | | X | |
| 65 | Body Isolations | | 73 | | | XX | | |
| 71 | Body Isolation Relays | | 79 | | X | XX | X | X |
| 74 | Body Parts Mini-Golf | | 82 | X | | XX | | |
| 81 | Bombardment | | 92 | X | | | XX | |
| 18 | Bounce Back | | 20 | XX | | | | X |
| 28 | Building Towers | | 30 | XX | | | X | |
| 6 | Bubble Pop | | 8 | XX | | X | | |

xx - Primary Emphasis
x - Secondary Emphasis

# Unit One: Motor Skills

**Title:** CIRCLE BALL

**Number: 1**

**Goal:** Increase hand-eye coordination skills.

**Objective:** Student will hit a ball moving in a circular direction three consecutive times.

**Environment:**
Indoors or outdoors.

**Appropriate For:**
Walkers or wheelchair participants.

**Number of Players:**
One to ten.

**Equipment:**
Stopwatch, tetherball, scoreboard.

**Teaching Hints:**

1. Attach screw eye overhead to ceiling.
2. Attach nylon cord or rope to tetherball.
3. Tie swivel hook to nylon cord or rope.
4. Hang swivel hook with nylon cord and tetherball to screw eye overhead.
5. Caution the students about sitting on the tetherball.

**Procedures:**

1. Divide the students into equal teams.
   *Example:* Ten students equal five teams.
2. Place each team member on opposite sides of the ball.
3. One-half of the team will be participating at any given moment.
4. As the teacher signals "GO" a team member swings the ball in a circular motion. The team partner tries to hit the ball as it is moving in a circular motion. Each hit scores one point. At the end of 30 seconds, 60 seconds, etc., the teacher signals "STOP."
5. Each team reports their total number of hits. The winning team is the team which scores the highest number of hits per set.

**Title:** CIRCLE SWING BALL

**Goal:** Improve perceptual motor skills.

**Objective:** Student will tap circling ball on three out of five rotations.

**Environment:**
Indoors.

**Appropriate For:**
Students with use of arms.

**Number of Players:**
Four to eight.

**Equipment:**
Circle, swinging ball.

**Teaching Hints:**

1. If ball loses momentum and falls to the center of the circle, no one may recover it except the teacher, who will then hand the ball to a new starter.

**Procedures:**

1. Students sit in a circle around a hanging ball.
2. Ball is started in circular motion by any player.
3. Students count how many times they can tap the ball around the circle without it going out of bounds (or out of reach).

**Diagram**

**Title:** LIKE ME | **Number: 3**

**Goal:** Improve catching and throwing skills.

**Objective:** Student will catch or throw a ball as the teacher does on three out of six attempts.

**Environment:**
Indoors or outdoors.

**Appropriate For:**
Walkers and wheelchairs.

**Number of Players:**
One to twelve.

**Equipment:**
Small balls (nerf balls, yarn balls, etc.) scoreboard, chalk.

**Teaching Hints:**
1. Draw a line for students to sit or stand on.
2. Mark a line five and ten feet from the students to vary the distance for throwing and catching.

**Procedures:**
1. Each time a student throws or catches a ball the same as the teacher they get one point.
2. The winner is the student with the most points.

| **Title:** PRINGLE DROP | **Number: 4** |
|---|---|

**Goal:** Improve perceptual motor skills.

**Objective:** Student will successfully drop three out of six ping pong balls into cans in 60 seconds.

| **Environment:** Indoors or outdoors. | **Appropriate For:** All students. |
|---|---|

| **Number of Players:** Six to twelve. | **Equipment:** Six to eight Pringle or tennis ball cans, six ping pong balls. |
|---|---|

**Teaching Hints:**

1. Cans can be adjusted to skill level; either right below the arm of the wheelchair for the very involved, or at a short distance for the more skilled.

2. Tennis ball cans can be used in place of Pringle cans.

3. Cans can be color coded, giving different values to the different colors.

4. Cans are set up in blocks so that no spaces are between cans.

**Procedures:**

1. Student is as near cans as necessary to guarantee some success.

2. Give different values to different colors.

3. Each student attempts to drop all six ping pong balls into the cans.

4. Points are awarded for each ball landing in a can.

**Title:** SOAPY SHUFFLE

**Goal:** Increase arm (leg) range of motion and strength.

**Objective:** Student will slide soap disc a distance of five feet on three out of five attempts.

**Environment:**

Indoors or outdoors.

**Appropriate For:**

Students with arm or leg use.

**Number of Players:**

Four per shuffle-board court.

**Equipment:**

Bars of soap (wrapped), paper diagram of shuffleboard court.

**Teaching Hints:**

1. Bars of soap are easy to hold, cheap and slide more like a real disc.
2. Shuffleboard court may be drawn directly on smooth floor with chalk or shoe polish.

**Procedures:**

1. Players stand or sit four feet from end of shuffle-board.
2. Each player gets two alternating turns.
3. If the bar of soap lands on a line the lower score is taken.
4. Until all areas are filled, no one may throw on an area that has a bar of soap.
5. After eight turns all scores are totaled and player with highest score is the winner.

**Diagram**

**Title:** BUBBLE POP

**Number: 6**

**Goal:** Improve perceptual motor skills.

**Objective:** Student will maintain sitting balance on T-stool for 30 seconds while popping bubble with two hands.

| Environment: | Appropriate For: |
|---|---|
| Indoors. | All students. |

| Number of Players: | Equipment: |
|---|---|
| Any number. | Bubble mixture, T-stools, or balance boards. |

**Teaching Hints:**

1. Activity good for midline remediation. Have student pop bubbles with a cross body pattern.

**Procedures:**

1. Students sit on T-stools, or stand in close circle.
2. Teacher blows bubbles for students and determines how that bubble should be popped. (*Example:* pop with two hands, one hand, head, nose, knee, foot, etc.)

**Title:** CARPET SQUARE GAMES

**Number: 7**

**Goal:** Increase visual discrimination skills.

**Objective:** Student will correctly identify the carpet square removed from the group in four out of five attempts.

**Environment:**
Indoors.

**Appropriate For:**
Ambulatory students.

**Number of Players:**
Groups of fifteen or less students.

**Equipment:**
Carpet squares or colored tape.

**Teaching Hints:**
CAUTION: The carpet squares can cause accidents for some students. If wheelchairs or students with walkers or crutches are going to play, use colored tape rather than carpet squares.

**Procedures:**
1. Each student has a carpet square.
2. Form a circle with squares on floor.
3. Skip or walk around carpet squares.
4. One person (teacher, aide, or volunteer) will turn his/her back on group, and at random intervals the person will clap his/her hands. This is a signal for students to find a carpet square and sit down. Music can be used instead of hand clap. When music is used one person with back to group will stop music as signal to sit down.
5. Remove one square each time. If student can not find carpet square to sit on, that student is out of game, or in "*mush pot*" for one turn.

**Variations:**
1. Small groups of five or six in circle. Have each student do *their thing* with carpet square. Encourage each student to do something different.
2. Students can place carpet squares under each knee or hands and knees and skate (hardwood or tile floors).
3. Carpet square relay race—skating on knees or all fours.

9

**Title:** BIG FIVE

**Number: 8**

**Goal:** Improve hand-eye coordination skills.

**Objective:** Student will catch a ball in three out of five attempts.

**Environment:**
Outdoors or indoors.

**Appropriate For:**
Students with limited useage of one or two arms.

**Number of Players:**
Two to five.

**Equipment:**
Yarn balls, nerf balls.

**Teaching Hints:**
1. Position the students facing away from the sun.
2. Draw number (1-5) in front of each student on the blacktop.
3. Use cue of "hands ready, look at me."

**Procedures:**
1. Teacher calls "ONE," looks at a number one, but throws to number five.
2. The student that catches five balls gets to move to number five.
3. The rotation continues as the students catch the ball. The winner is the student who stays on number five the longest.

**Title:** NERF TAG

**Number: 9**

**Goal:** Improve throwing skills.

**Objective:** Student will successfully hit target with eight-inch nerf ball in three out of five attempts.

**Environment:**
Grassy outdoor area.

**Appropriate For:**
Students with some use of arms.

**Number of Players:**
Any number.

**Equipment:**
Eight-inch nerf ball or nerf frisbee.

**Teaching Hints:**
1. The nerf frisbee requires a slightly higher degree of skill.

**Procedures:**
1. Students are taken out of chairs and spread out inside a ropped off 20 x 20 foot area.
2. One student is designated as IT.
3. IT attempts to tag other players by hitting the player with the nerf ball.
4. Any player hit by the nerf ball then becomes IT.
5. Players may not cross over the rope.

**Diagram**

**Title:** POPPING BUTTONS

**Number: 10**

**Goal:** Improve fine motor skills and hand control.

**Objective:** Student will shoot button with thumb and first finger into five-point zone five out of ten attempts.

**Environment:**
Indoors or outdoors.

**Appropriate For:**
All students.

**Number of Players:**
Any number.

**Equipment:**
Ten large, flat buttons per student.

**Teaching Hints:**

**Procedures:**

1. Mark out court with masking tape.
2. Each student is given ten buttons.
3. Student attempts to toss or snap button onto wall.
4. Buttons rebound off wall and land in one of the court areas.
5. Score is determined by totalling court points for all ten buttons.
6. Player with highest total wins.

**Diagram**

**Title:** BARREL HOCKEY

**Goal:** Improve perceptual motor skills.

**Objective:** Student will hit ball into barrel, placed at five feet, three out of five attempts.

**Environment:**
Indoors or outdoors.

**Appropriate For:**
Students with use of at least one arm.

**Number of Players:**
Four to twelve.

**Equipment:**
Hockey sticks, wiffle balls, ice cream cartons.

**Teaching Hints:**

**Procedures:**

1. Each student has own stick and ball.
2. Cartons are placed in front of students and adjusted for abilities to insure some success.
3. On teacher's cue, student attempts to get ball in barrel in the least number of hits.
4. Hits are totalled and high score wins.

**Variation:**

1. Cartons are placed in a semicircle and given different point values.
2. Student aims and hits wiffle ball into barrels and is awarded appropriate points.
3. Student with highest cumulative points after five shots is winner.

**Diagram**

13

**Title:** BEAN BAG BARREL

**Goal:** Improve throwing skills.

**Objective:** Student will throw three out of five bean bags into a barrel.

**Environment:**
Indoors or outdoors.

**Appropriate For:**
Students with some arm use.

**Number of Players:**
Any number.

**Equipment:**
Bean bags, large ice cream cartons.

**Teaching Hints:**

1. Cartons may be given different point values. The farthest has the highest value.
2. Values may be readjusted according to students' skill levels.

**Procedures:**

1. Place at least six ice cream cartons approximately ten feet from each other forming a large circle area.
2. Mark a throwing line eight feet (or appropriate distance for skill level) from cartons. Players stand behind throwing line with toes or wheels touching line.
3. The first player starts at throwing line and throws his/her five bean bags, one at a time, attempting to have each fall completely within the ice cream carton area. Bean bags that remain lodged on the edge of a wall partition score half point.
4. When the first player has thrown all his/her bean bags the bags are collected and the second player tries. Play continues for balance of players.

**Diagram**

**Title:** WALL BATTLE

**Number: 13**

**Goal:** Improve hand-eye coordination skills.

**Objective:** Student will catch a thrown ball in three out of five attempts.

**Environment:**

Outdoors.

**Appropriate For:**

Ambulatory students.

**Number of Players:**

Two or more.

**Equipment:**

Beach ball or small playground ball.

**Teaching Hints:**

1. Draw a mark with chalk high on the wall for a focal point to put the ball in proper alignment for opposite player.

**Procedures:**

1. Draw a line five feet, ten feet and fifteen feet from the wall.
2. Position students on five-foot line.
3. Student A throws ball at the wall with two hands trying to bounce the ball off the wall so that partner B can catch the ball.
4. Partner B returns the ball in the same manner.

**Diagram**

////////// Wall //////////

5' _____
            A       B

10' _____

15' _____

| **Title:** BLOCK DOWN | **Number: 14** |
|---|---|

**Goal:** Improve throwing skills for distance and accuracy.

**Objective:** Students will throw a ball and knock down an object three out of five tries.

| **Environment:** Outdoors or indoors. | **Appropriate For:** All students. |
|---|---|

| **Number of Players:** One to twelve. | **Equipment:** Elementary blocks, small balls, nerf balls. |
|---|---|

**Teaching Hints:**

1. Set blocks up on table, level with the heads of students.
2. Mark the blocks with numbers, letters or colors.
3. Position the students in a semi-circle or line formation facing the blocks.
4. Place the table near a divider or wall.

**Procedures:**

1. Position the students five to ten feet from the table.
2. Each student calls a number, letter or color and throws the ball towards that block.
3. The winner is the student that has the highest number, most letters, or most colors.

**Title:** READY-HANDS

**Goal:** Improve hand-eye coordination skills.

**Objective:** Student will catch three out of five balls from a distance of five to ten feet.

**Environment:**

Outdoors or indoors.

**Appropriate For:**

All students.

**Number of Players:**

Two to six.

**Equipment:**

Small balls, yarn balls, nerf balls.

**Teaching Hints:**

1. Vary the distance of the throw depending on the student.
2. A ball which lands on the lap and arms for a wheelchair student can count.

**Procedures:**

1. Space students equal distances apart.
2. The teacher says "READY-HANDS."
3. The teacher makes eye contact with a student but throws the ball to another student.
4. If the ball is caught by the student, the student has one catch to his/her credit.
5. Each student keeps his/her own score.
6. Continue to ask students what their total score is.

**Title:** DISTANCE PITCH

**Number: 16**

**Goal:** Improve throwing skills.

**Objective:** Student will throw a tennis ball a distance of 10 feet.

**Environment:**
Outdoors.

**Appropriate For:**
Students with arm and shoulder mobility.

**Number of Players:**
One to ten.

**Equipment:**
Yarn ball, tennis ball, softball.

**Teaching Hints:**
1. Vary the distance according to the abilities of the students.
2. A twenty-foot throw could be worth five points.

**Procedures:**
1. Divide students into two teams.
2. Each time a student throws a ball 10 feet, he or she scores one point for their team.
3. The team with the most points wins the game.

**Diagram**

20 ft.————————— (Five Points) —————————

15 ft.——————————————————————

10 ft.————————— (One Point) —————————

5 ft.——————————————————————

A A A A A      B B B B B

| **Title:** SWING ALONG | **Number: 17** |
| --- | --- |

**Goal:** Increase hand-eye coordination skills.

**Objective:** Student will catch a swinging object within 10 seconds.

**Environment:**
Indoors or outdoors.

**Appropriate For:**
Walkers and wheelchair participants.

**Number of Players:**
One to ten.

**Equipment:**
Stopwatch, tetherballs, scoreboard.

**Teaching Hints:**
1. Attach screw eye overhead to ceiling.
2. Attach nylon cord or rope to tetherball.
3. Tie swivel hook to nylon cord or rope.
4. Hang swivel hook with nylon cord and tetherball to screw eye overhead.
5. Caution the students about sitting on the tetherball.

**Procedures:**
1. Divide the students into equal teams.
   *Example:* Ten students equal five teams.
2. Place each team member on both sides of the ball.
3. The teacher signals ''GO.'' Each team member swings and catches the ball.
4. Each catch is counted. At the end of 30 seconds, 60 seconds, etc., the teacher signals ''STOP.''
5. Each team reports their total number of catches. The winning team is the team which scores the highest number of catches. The winning team gets one point.

**Title:** BOUNCE BACK

**Number: 18**

**Goal:** Improve throwing, catching and ball handling skills.

**Objective:** Students will throw a ball against a pitchback and catch it three out of five times.

**Environment:**

Indoors or outdoors.

**Appropriate For:**

Walkers and wheelchairs.

**Number of Players:**

One to twelve.

**Equipment:**

Small balls (tennis balls, six-inch playground balls), bean bags.

**Teaching Hints:**

1. Give a ball or bean bag to each student.
2. Draw a line for the students to stand on.
3. Select an aide or assistant to hold the pitchback.

**Procedures:**

1. Divide students into two teams.
2. Position students at appropriate distance from the pitchback.
3. Each successful throw and catch is equal to two points: one point for the throw and one point for the catch.
4. After each student has had a turn, the points are totaled to see who has the most points between each team.
5. The winning team is the team that has the most total points.

| **Title:** LETTER EXCHANGE | **Number: 19** |
|---|---|

**Goal:** Improve mobility and listening skills.

**Objective:** Students will exchange places with another student three out of five times without being tagged.

**Environment:**
Outdoors.

**Appropriate For:**
All students.

**Number of Players:**
Four to thirty.

**Equipment:**
None.

**Teaching Hints:**

1. Draw as many letters on the blacktop or cement as there are students.

2. If a wheelchair student becomes IT, move him or her closer to other students.

**Procedures:**

1. Teacher selects IT.

2. IT calls two letters who are to exchange places with one another.

3. IT becomes the tagger and tries to tag one of the students exchanging places with another letter.

4. IT cannot go to a vacant letter.

5. The student that is tagged becomes IT.

**Diagram**

**Title:** THREE-MINUTE STACK ATTACK

**Number: 20**

**Goal:** Improve hand-eye coordination skills.

**Objective:** Students will roll a ball five feet and knock down a stack of blocks three out of five times in three minutes.

| Environment: | Appropriate For: |
|---|---|
| Indoors or outdoors. | All students. |

| Number of Players: | Equipment: |
|---|---|
| Two to six. | Elementary building blocks, small balls, stopwatch |

**Teaching Hints:**

1. Set the game up on a table if a child must be in a wheelchair and cannot be positioned on the floor.
2. Position the students in a semicircle.
3. Position a helper in back of the blocks to catch the ball and set up the blocks.

**Procedures:**

1. Divide the group of six children into two teams.
2. Each team member rolls the ball trying to knock down the stack of blocks.
3. On the signal "GO" each team has three minutes to known down all the stacks of blocks on their side.
4. The first team that knocks down all the blocks gets one point for their side.
5. The team with the most points wins the game.

**Title:** SAUCER TOSS

**Goal:** Improve hand-eye accuracy skills.

**Objective:** Students will throw a bean bag on to a pre-selected number in two out of four tries.

**Environment:**

Indoors or outdoors.

**Appropriate For:**

Walkers and students in wheelchairs.

**Number of Players:**

Two to twelve.

**Equipment:**

Ten saucers (pie tins), fifty bean bags, small chalkboard.

**Teaching Hints:**

1. Arrange the saucers in a circular arrangement with the highest numbers in the middle.

2. Select an aide or helper to assist giving the bean bags back.

3. If the activity is too slow, put one-half of the students into another circle.

**Procedures:**

1. Divide students into two teams. One team is designated "*odd number*" and the other team is designated "*even number.*"

2. Each student calls four numbers and throws the bean bags at the numbers. If the bean bag goes into the saucer, that student scores those points for their team.

3. Pick up the bean bags and give them back to the students after the throws have been made.

4. The team that scores the most points wins the game.

**Diagram**

**Title:** BALLOONICS

**Number: 22**

**Goal:** Improve hand-eye coordination skills.

**Objective:** Students will catch a balloon three out of five times without a visible cue from the thrower.

**Environment:**
Indoors.

**Appropriate For:**
Walkers and students with limited upper body strength.

**Number of Players:**
Two.

**Equipment:**
Small portable room divider, large round balloons.

**Teaching Hints:**

1. Emphasize throwing the baloon to the left and right of the opponent.

**Procedures:**

1. Sitting in chairs, two students face one another, separated by a divider.

2. Student A, sitting below the top of the divider, lets the balloon go toward his partner five times.

3. Student B must catch the balloon three out of five times.

4. After five attempts, student B throws the balloon to student A who tries to catch the balloon five times.

5. The winner is the student that catches the balloon the most number of times.

**Title:** BAG-IT                                                    **Number: 23**

**Goal:** Improve hand-eye accuracy and physical endurance.

**Objective:** Students will throw a bean bag and hit a specific target on three out of five attempts in one minute.

**Environment:**
Gymnasium or outdoors.

**Appropriate For:**
Wheelchair students and slow walkers.

**Number of Players:**
Four to twelve.

**Equipment:**
Chalk, five bean bags for each student, stopwatch.

**Teaching Hints:**

1. Draw a two-foot diameter circle.
2. The sixty-second stopwatch count starts when IT reaches ten.
3. Select a new IT every sixty-second period.

**Procedures:**

1. Give each student five bean bags.
2. Select a student to be IT. IT positions himself or herself inside the circle.
3. IT covers his or her eyes and counts to ten by ones, while the other players scatter within the specified boundary.
4. Upon reaching the number ten, IT must move outside the circle.
5. Each student has sixty seconds to throw his or her bean bags into the circle. Each bean bag thrown inside the circle scores one point for each student. The student with the most points wins the sixty-second round.
6. IT tries to "Bag-IT" or knock down the bean bags thrown toward the circle.

**Diagram**

**Title:** BOARD BALL

**Goal:** Improve throwing accuracy skills.

**Objective:** Students will throw a ball and hit a letter on a board five out of ten times.

**Environment:**

Outdoors or indoors.

**Appropriate For:**

All students.

**Number of Players:**

One to thirty.

**Equipment:**

Tennis balls or nerf balls, stopwatch.

**Teaching Hints:**

1. Give each student several balls.

2. Record a score from each team at the end of each two-minute period (or round).

3. Place large barrels at the bottom of the board to catch the balls.

**Procedures:**

1. Divide students into two or more teams.

2. Select a student to be "*Captain*" of each team and call the student's name to throw the ball.

3. Each student throws the ball at a letter on the board. If the ball hits the letter, the student scores one point for his or her team.

4. The team with the highest score wins the game.

**Diagram**

**Title:** WATER BASKETBALL

**Number: 25**

**Goal:** Improve throwing accuracy.

**Objective:** Student will throw three out of eight balls into water containers.

**Environment:**
Outdoors.

**Appropriate For:**
Students with use of one arm.

**Number of Players:**
One to ten.

**Equipment:** Small plastic pool, gallon Purex containers with the top cut off, four-inch balls.

**Teaching Hints:**

**Procedures:**

1. Fill small pool with water. Float the Purex containers on top of the water.
2. Students sit around the pool at distances appropriate for skill level.
3. Each student receives five balls (ping-pong balls may be used in place of four-inch balls).
4. Students take turns attempting to throw the balls into the floating containers.
5. Each container may be worth one point. Different point values may be given to each container.
6. Player with highest total points wins.

**Title:** STICK-BALL RELAY | **Number: 26**

**Goal:** Improve perceptual motor skills.

**Objective:** Student will hit ball around cone placed at a distance of 25 feet in one minute.

**Environment:**
Outdoors—grassy area or blacktop.

**Appropriate For:**
Students with use of at least one arm.

**Number of Players:**
Six to ten.

**Equipment:** Two small balls (tennis or hand balls), two posts or cones, sticks (broom handles) or bats.

**Teaching Hints:**

1. May be used for students in wheelchairs.
2. Try to divide teams into two teams with students of equal abilities.

**Procedures:**

1. Mark starting line.
2. Drive posts in ground about 25 feet from starting line.
3. Players line up single file behind starting line. Each team is given a stick and a ball. Ball is placed on ground at starting line. First player in line is given stick.
4. At the GO signal, the first player hits the ball along the ground, around the post, then back to the starting line. The stick is then given to the second player and that player proceeds to do as the first player.
5. This is continued until all players have finished hitting the ball around the post and back.
6. The first team that gets all players through the course and back to the starting line is the winner.

**Title:** TRI BALL

**Goal:** Increase throwing and catching skills.

**Objective:** Student will catch and throw a ball at least five times in the outfield while the UP student travels around the bases.

**Environment:**
Outdoors.

**Appropriate For:**
All students.

**Number of Players:**
Five to ten.

**Equipment:**
Yarn ball, three bases (home base, first base and second base).

**Teaching Hints:**

1. Points can be scored only by the team in the outfield.
2. After each team has had one turn each at being UP a rotation is made.

**Procedures:**

1. Divide the students into two teams.
2. Standing on home base, the child designated as UP throws the ball into the field and walks, runs, or wheels to first base and continues on to second base and back to home base.
3. The team in the outfield gets points each time a successful throw and catch is made in the outfield.

**Title:** BUILDING TOWERS

**Goal:** Improve ball handling skills.

**Objective:** Student will roll a ball along a straight line for a distance of five feet.

| Environment: | Appropriate For: |
|---|---|
| Indoors or outdoors. | All students. |

| Number of Players: | Equipment: |
|---|---|
| One to ten. | Elementary building blocks, small balls or large balls. |

**Teaching Hints:**

1. Build the tower lower than the student's head.

2. Vary the activity by having the students roll the ball through the bottom of the tower. The objective would be to roll the ball *through* the tower without knocking it down.

**Procedures:**

1. Position the children sitting in a circle approximately 15 feet in diameter.

2. Set blocks up in the middle of the circle.

3. Select a student to build part of the tower or give an idea where the blocks should be placed.

4. Pass out balls to all the students.

5. Selecting one child at a time, the student rolls or bounces the ball to see if they can knock the tower down.

**Diagram**

Tower

| **Title:** ROLL-A-SCORE | **Number: 29** |
|---|---|

**Goal:** Improve ball handling skills.

**Objective:** Student will roll a ball and score a point on three out of five attempts.

| **Environment:** Outdoors or indoors. | **Appropriate For:** All students. |
|---|---|

| **Number of Players:** Two to ten. | **Equipment:** Blocks, large balls. |
|---|---|

**Teaching Hints:**

1. Use any appropriate color of blocks.
2. Vary the activity to allow bouncing the ball.
3. Position an aide on the sidelines to get the balls.
4. Use one ball at a time.
5. Place the blocks in the middle of a rectangle.

**Procedures:**

1. Divide players into two teams. Position each team facing each other at opposite ends of a rectangle.
2. One team is designated the REDS.
   One team is designated the BLUES.
3. The object of the game is for the red team to knock down the red blocks, and the blue team to knock down the blue blocks.
4. The first team to knock down all of its colored blocks first scores one point.

**Diagram**

Blue Team (B blocks on left) — Red Team (R blocks on right)

**Title:** WALL BALL

**Number: 30**

**Goal:** Improve throwing accuracy skills.

**Objective:** Student will throw a ball and hit a moving player two out of five attempts.

| Environment: | Appropriate For: |
|---|---|
| Outdoors. | All students. |

| Number of Players: | Equipment: |
|---|---|
| Two to ten. | Yarn ball or small playground ball, nerf ball, chalk. |

**Teaching Hints:**

1. Draw a line with chalk three feet from the wall. (This is called the "wall line.")
2. Draw a line with chalk fifteen feet from the wall line. (This is called the "back line.")
3. Vary the distance of the lines according to the abilities of the students.

**Procedures:**

1. Divide the players into two teams.
2. Team A stands/sits three feet from the wall.
3. Team B stands/sits on the back line.
4. Team B throws the ball at Team A. If a member of Team A is hit with the ball, Team B scores one point.
5. Each team scores three points and changes positions.
6. The winner is the team which can score the most points in a given time period.

**Diagram**

```
///////////////Wall//////////////
```
Wall Line ——————————————
　　　　　　　　　　Team A


Back Line ——————————————
　　　　　　　　　　Team B

32

**Title:** TARGET BALL

**Number: 31**

**Goal:** Improve hand-eye accuracy and throwing skills.

**Objective:** Student will throw and bounce a ball and score five points on each throw.

**Environment:**

Outdoors or indoors.

**Appropriate For:**

Students with use of at least one arm.

**Number of Players:**

Two to ten.

**Equipment:**

Chalk, target, any size small balls, chalk board.

**Teaching Hints:**

1. Position the students two feet in back of circle #1.
2. Position aides (helpers) around the circle to catch the balls.

**Procedures:**

1. Divide students into two equal teams; Team A and Team B.
2. Students sit or stand on designated number with their team.
3. Alternating turns, each team player throws a ball into the circle.
4. Each player attempts to score five points on each throw. The ball must land between the lines to score a point.
5. The winning team is the team that scores the most points in 20 minutes.

**Diagram**

33

**Title:** NUMBER SOCCER

**Number: 32**

**Goal:** Improve wheelchair mobility and kicking skills.

**Objective:** Move, push or kick a ball over opponent's goal line within one minute.

**Environment:**

Outdoors.

**Appropriate For:**

Walkers and wheelchair participants.

**Number of Players:**

Four to twenty.

**Equipment:**

One soccer ball and one cageball.

**Teaching Hints:**

1. As each student is selected for a team have them stand on a number.
2. Use the signal "*freeze*" to stop all action at any time.
3. More than one student number can be called.
4. Give "*bonus points*" to the team which has all its players back to their own goal line before the other team.

**Procedures:**

1. Divide students into two teams.
2. Each student stands, wheels or sits over a number.
3. The teacher calls a number and each student walks, wheels or moves to the center of the playing area.
4. Each student moves, pushes or kicks the ball towards the opponent's goal line.
5. The team that moves the ball over the opponent's goal line first scores a point for their side.

**Diagram**

**Title:** DODGE BALL HIT

**Goal:** Increase throwing and bouncing ball skills.

**Objective:** Student will throw or bounce a ball at another student in the circle, contacting that student two out of five times.

**Environment:**
Outdoors—blacktop area.

**Appropriate For:**
Walkers and wheelchair participants.

**Number of Players:**
Four to twenty.

**Equipment:**
Yarn balls, nerf balls, or small 8-inch diameter playground balls.

**Teaching Hints:**

1. Use a soft ball.
2. Use two balls occasionally.
3. Continue to add players to center of circle.
4. Allow wheelchair participants to bend over and use their wheelchair for cover.

**Procedures:**

1. Students stand or sit in a circle formation.
2. Teacher selects a student to be inside the circle.
3. Students standing on the circle throw or bounce the ball toward the students moving around inside the circle.
4. The student hit by the ball returns to the outside of the circle.
5. The student throwing the ball moves to the inside of the circle.
6. Each thrower that has previously thrown must give the ball to a student that has not thrown.

**Title:** BACK AWAY

**Goal:** Improve hand-eye coordination skills.

**Objective:** Students will catch and throw a ball continuously for one minute six out of ten times.

**Environment:**
Indoors or outdoors.

**Appropriate For:**
Walkers and wheelchairs.

**Number of Players:**
Two to twenty.

**Equipment:**
Small and large balls, stopwatch.

**Teaching Hints:**
1. Position students so they start two feet apart.
2. Position helpers or aides with the students who need the most help with throwing and catching skills.

**Procedures:**
1. Divide students into pairs.
2. Students begin the game facing each other approximately two feet apart.
3. Each time a successful catch is made the student moves backward one foot.
4. On the signal GO each team of partners begins to catch and throw balls.
5. The team which is farthest apart at the end of one minute gets a point.
6. The team which scores the most points at the end of the game is the winner.

**Title:** FACE AROUND

**Goal:** Improve hand-eye accuracy skills.

**Objective:** Student will throw a ball and hit six out of twelve parts of the face upon teacher's request in three minutes.

**Environment:**
Indoors or outdoors.

**Appropriate For:**
Students in kindergarten and primary grades.

**Number of Players:**
Two to twelve.

**Equipment:**
Butcher paper, felt pen, nerf balls, stopwatch.

**Teaching Hints:**
1. Draw two large faces on butcher paper.
2. Review the body parts of the face with the students.
3. Position students five to ten feet from the butcher paper.
4. Hang butcher paper eye level with the students.
5. Have a helper sit near the face to give the balls back to students.

**Procedures:**
1. Divide students into two teams.
2. The teacher names a part of the face and the student throws the ball at that part on the drawing.
3. On the signal GO each team tries to hit six or more body parts on the face.
4. Each student gets one throw before giving the ball to another teammate.
5. The winner is the team which can hit the most facial body parts in three minutes.

**Title:** KICKAROO

**Goal:** Improve eye-foot accuracy.

**Objective:** Students will kick a ball three out of five times between cones in two minutes.

| Environment: | Appropriate For: |
|---|---|
| Outdoors. | Walkers. |

| Number of Players: | Equipment: |
|---|---|
| Five per team. | Two cones, five medium size balls, chalk, rope. |

**Teaching Hints:**

1. Divide students into teams with five players on each team.
2. Rotate the students so that each student has a responsibility:
   a. kicker
   b. goalie
   c. retriever
   d. ball handler
   e. judge
3. Emphasize that the ball must stay lower than the goalie's head.
4. The goalie can block the ball with the hands.

**Procedures:**

1. On the signal GO the student in the number one position kicks the ball five times trying to score five points in two minutes.
2. Each student moves to the next highest number; number five moves to number one position.
3. The winner at the end of the period is the student who has the greatest number of points or balls kicked on the ground between the cones.

**Diagram**

Retriever
1
○————————○

Goalie
2
————————————

Kicker
3
————————————

○ ○ ○ ○
Ball Handler
5

Judge
4

| | |
|---|---|
| **Title:**  HOCKEY HIT FOR DISTANCE | **Number: 37** |

**Goal:**  Improve perceptual motor skills.

**Objective:**  Student will hit a whiffle ball a distance of 15 feet in four out of five attempts.

**Environment:**
Outdoors—cement area.

**Appropriate For:**
Students with at least some use of arms.

**Number of Players:**
Any number.

**Equipment:**
Hockey sticks, whiffle balls and chalk.

**Teaching Hints:**

**Procedures:**

1. Students are paired off. Each pair receives a hockey stick and two whiffle balls.
2. Cement area is marked off into point areas of 5, 10, 15 and 20.
3. Each partner takes two turns. All distances are recorded and totaled up after designated time period has ended.
4. Team with most points wins.

**Diagram**

20 _____ 20

15 _____ 15

10 _____ 10

5 _____ 5

**Starting**
**Line** _____
          X    X    X    X    X    X

**Title:** KICK AND GO

**Number: 38**

**Goal:** Improve foot-eye coordination skills.

**Objective:** Student will kick a ball three out of five times and run 25 yards in 45 seconds.

| Environment: | Appropriate For: |
|---|---|
| Outdoors. | Walkers and students in wheelchairs. |

| Number of Players: | Equipment: |
|---|---|
| One to twelve. | Stopwatch. |

**Teaching Hints:**

1. Set up three or more running stations.
2. Select an aide to be scorekeeper.
3. Let the student walk back to the starting line after racing.

**Procedures:**

1. Kick stationary ball 10 feet and run 25 yards without stopping.
2. On the signal GO each student kicks the ball and runs.
3. One point is scored for kicking the ball and each student scores one, two, or three additional points depending on which place they finish.
4. The winner is the team with the most points.

| **Title:** FIRST AND HOME | **Number: 39** |
|---|---|

**Goal:** Improve hand-eye coordination skills.

**Objective:** Students will hit a ball with a bat on three out of five pitches.

| **Environment:** Outdoors. | **Appropriate For:** Students in wheelchairs and walkers. |
|---|---|

| **Number of Players:** One to twelve. | **Equipment:** Plastic bats. |
|---|---|

**Teaching Hints:**

1. Use a batting-T for additional help.
2. Bounce the ball in front of the plate before the student swings the bat.
3. Caution the student to lay the bat down gently on the ground after hitting the ball.
4. Vary the distance between home and first base, depending on the limitations of the students.

**Procedures:**

1. Select two teams.
2. Team A is positioned in the outfield.
3. Each student receives five pitches.
4. On the last pitch, the batter runs, or wheels, to first base and back to home plate before the ball is returned to the pitcher.
5. If the batter returns "*home*," he or she scores one point for their team.

# Unit Two: Physical Fitness

| | |
|---|---|
| **Title:** BALLOON SLAP | **Number: 40** |

**Goal:** Improve perceptual motor skills.

**Objective:** Student will contact suspended balloon with hand or stick 30 times in 60 seconds.

| **Environment:** | **Appropriate For:** |
|---|---|
| Indoors or outdoors. | All students. |

| **Number of Players:** | **Equipment:** |
|---|---|
| Four to twelve. | Balloons, yard, elastic cord. |

**Teaching Hints:**

1. Have students pair up and take alternate turns.

**Procedures:**

1. Each student is placed in front of a large balloon suspended from a piece of yarn by an elastic cord.
2. Students try to hit (make contact with) balloon as many times as possible in a certain length of time. *For example:* 60 seconds.
3. Greatest number of hits within time frame wins.

**Variations:**

1. Put sand inside balloon to make it heavier.
2. Have students hit balloon with a rhythm stick.
3. Blindfold students and put a bell in each balloon.

| **Title:** FINGER POPS | **Number: 41** |
|---|---|

**Goal:** Improve fine motor control.

**Objective:** Student will pop three out of five finger pops into target box placed at three feet.

| **Environment:** Indoors or outdoors. | **Appropriate For:** All students. |
|---|---|

| **Number of Players:** Any number. | **Equipment:** Commercially made finger pops. |
|---|---|

**Teaching Hints:**

**Procedures:**

**Activity #1**

1. Students sit in circle with ice cream barrel placed in center.
2. Each student gets five finger pops. Each pop that goes into the barrel is five points.
3. Student with most points wins.

**Activity #2**

1. Same as above except each student has his/her own barrel at which to shoot.

**Activity #3**

1. Finger pop battle: Students form teams and attempt to hit players on other team with finger pops.
2. Each hit is worth one point. Team with most hits wins.

**Title:** WHEEL-WALK-RUN | **Number: 42**

**Goal:** Improve cardiovascular fitness.

**Objective:** Wheel, walk or run 10, 25 or 50 yards in a given time period.

**Environment:**
Outdoors, blacktop, running lanes.

**Appropriate For:**
Wheelchair and ambulatory students.

**Number of Players:**
One to twenty.

**Equipment:**
Stop watch.

**Teaching Hints:**
1. Wheelchair participants can have a pusher if needed.
2. Vary the distance of the races. Include 10-yard race, 25-yard race, and a 50-yard race. Keep the scores separate.
3. There can be a winner for each separate race.

**Procedures:**
1. Divide students into two teams.
2. Each team member stands or sits at the starting line.
3. On the signal GO the students wheel, walk or run toward the finish line.
4. Record individual times.
5. Add the total individual seconds for a total team score.
6. The winner is the student with the highest individual score.

| **Title:** GRASS EXERCISE | **Number: 43** |

**Goal:** Improve gross motor fitness.

**Objective:** Student will independently demonstrate three exercises from grass exercise program.

**Environment:**
Outdoor—grassy area.

**Appropriate For:**
All students.

**Number of Players:**
Any number.

**Equipment:**
None.

**Teaching Hints:**
Students are taken out of chairs and placed supine on grass. Be careful of sun in eyes, wet grass and grass allergies. Students enjoy being free from the confines of their wheelchairs, and also being outside exercising rather than indoors on mats.

**Procedures:**
The following are suggested exercises that require little coordination or skill:

1. *Supine Stretch*—lying supine, students stretch cross laterally.
2. *Ladder Stretch*—lying supine, students stretch as they would climb a ladder.
   *Example:* Arms over head on grass, alternate pulling.
3. *Reach for the Sky*—lying supine, students stretch arms to sky, pull sky to their chest and hug the sky.
4. *Side Stretch*—lying supine, students bend at waist so as to touch fingertips to knee. Repeat both sides.
5. *Neck Warm-up*—lying supine, students lift head to 90°. Repeat to each side.
6. *Leg Reach*—lying supine, students lift one straight leg to sky. Repeat with other leg.
7. *Leg Crossover*—lying supine, students lift one leg up, cross it over other leg so as to touch grass, back to sky and down. Repeat with other leg.
8. *Knee Hugging*—lying supine, students bring knees to chest and hug them.
9. *Prone Flyer*—lying prone, students raise arms and legs at the same time.
10. *Back Extension*—lying prone, students extend chest, neck and head up as far as possible.

**Title:** SCOOTER BOARD RACES

**Goal:** Improve perceptual and sensory motor skills.

**Objective:** Student will cross laterally and locomote self on scooter board for a distance of 10 feet within 15 seconds.

**Environment:** Outdoors.

**Appropriate For:** Students with upper body control.

**Number of Players:** Two to ten.

**Equipment:** Scooter board, cones.

**Procedures:**

1. Determine a starting and racing distance (10-20 feet).
2. Determine method of locomotion, e.g., supine pushing with hands cross laterally, sitting on board using feet, and other variations.
3. At the GO signal students move themselves toward the finish line. The first student to cross finish line is winner.

**Diagram**

**Teaching Hints:**

1. Students can wear gloves to protect their hands from rough or hot outdoor surfaces.
2. Each student can be individually timed and scores compared.
3. Students can be divided into teams. Add up the total time of each team.

**Start**

**Finish**

**Title:** BLOW STATIONS #1—BOTTLE BLOW

**Number: 45**

**Goal:** Improve respiratory efficiency.

**Objective:** Student will displace at least one inch of water from one bottle to the next within three minutes.

**Environment:**
Indoors.

**Appropriate For:**
Students with voluntary breath control.

**Number of Players:**
Any number but not more than four per station.

**Equipment:**
Two jars, small plastic hose, water, rubbing alcohol.

**Teaching Hints:**
1. Clean plastic hose with alcohol between each turn.

**Procedures:**
1. First student attempts to blow all the water out of the first jar into second jar.
2. Score can either be time used to transfer water into second jar or the amount of water displaced within a given time (thirty seconds).
3. Each student repeats process.
4. Fastest time or most water displaced wins.

**Diagram**

Student Blows In Here

Plastic Hose

Copper Pipes

Water

**Title:** BLOW STATIONS #2—BLOW HOCKEY

**Number: 46**

**Goal:** Improve respiratory efficiency.

**Objective:** Student will score three goals (with no opponent) from center starting line within one minute.

**Environment:**
Indoors.

**Appropriate For:**
Students with voluntary breath control.

**Number of Players:**
Any number but not more than four per station.

**Equipment:**
Ping-pong balls, tape, straws, table.

**Teaching Hints:**

**Procedures:**

1. Two or four students sit facing each other across a 20-inch table. Table is marked with tape per diagram.
2. Ping-pong ball is placed on midline in circle to start game.
3. Both teams begin blowing to get ball through other team's goal.
4. Students may use straws if they have trouble localizing their breathing.
5. No hands or body parts may be used.
6. One point is scored for each goal.

**Diagram**

20'

**Title:** BLOW STATIONS #3—BLOW TRACK

**Goal:** Improve respiratory efficiency.

**Objective:** Student will keep ping-pong ball on opponent's side for at least seven seconds.

**Environment:**
Indoors.

**Appropriate For:**
Students with voluntary breath control.

**Number of Players:**
Any number but not more than four per station.

**Equipment:**
Ping-pong balls, track.

**Teaching Hints:**
1. Assign third student to keep score since points accumulate very quickly.

**Procedures:**
1. Two players position themselves at either end of ping-pong track.
2. Ball is placed on midline to start game.
3. Each player tries to blow ball into other player's half.
4. A point is scored each time the ball crosses the midline.
5. Player with most points after three minutes wins.

**Diagram**

**Title:** BLOW STATIONS #4—BIG BLOW

**Goal:** Improve respiratory efficiency.

**Objective:** Student will blow a ping-pong ball a distance of three feet on a single blow in three out of five attempts.

**Environment:**
Indoors.

**Appropriate For:**
Students with voluntary breath control.

**Number of Players:**
Any number but not more than four per station.

**Equipment:**
Ping-pong balls, tape, side boards (1'' x 1'' x 5').

**Teaching Hints:**

**Procedures:**

1. Use track as diagrammed below.
2. Each student gets five blows.
3. The longest distance of the five blows is recorded.
4. The next student takes turn and process is repeated until each student has had at least three turns to blow five times.
5. The total distances of the longest distance of each blow is figured and student with highest total wins.

**Diagram**

53

**Title:** BLOW STATIONS #5—BLOW RELAY

**Goal:** Improve respiratory efficiency.

**Objective:** Student will blow a ping-pong ball a distance of five feet within 15 seconds.

**Environment:**
Indoors.

**Appropriate For:**
Students with voluntary breath control.

**Number of Players:**
Any number but not more than four per station.

**Equipment:**
Ping-pong balls, tape, side boards (1'' x 1'' x 5').

**Teaching Hints:**

**Procedures:**

1. Students choose partners and line up single file behind starting line.
2. On signal, first partner blows ball along five-five track until ball hits stopping block, then returns ball (by blowing) to starting line.
3. Next partner repeats process.
4. First team to complete process wins.

**Diagram**

1-inch Sideboard

5'

**Title:** BALLOON VOLLEY BALL

**Goal:** Improve perceptual motor skills.

**Objective:** Student will make contact with a 12-inch tossed balloon on three out of five attempts.

**Environment:**
Indoors.

**Appropriate For:**
Physically handicapped.

**Number of Players:**
Any number.

**Equipment:**
Chairs, balloon, net or substitute (wedges).

**Teaching Hints:**

1. Use a 16'' rubberized balloon. (Lasts approximately two months blown up.)

   Can be ordered from:

   Reed Sammonds, Inc.
   Box 32
   Brookfield, Illinois 60513

**Procedures:**

1. All players must be seated and remain seated in wheelchairs or regular chairs at all times.

2. Unlimited number of hits on either side of net.

3. Spotters may tap balloon back in play.

4. Each team may have a coach seated in a movable chair behind his team to field the long ones that go over the heads of players in the back row. The coach may tap the balloon back into play for his team.

5. Players unable to use arm or use any body part may be assisted by teachers or aides.

6. Serve moves each time to next player. *Only* the serving team can score.

7. Point is scored when balloon hits floor on non-serving team's side of net.

8. Balloon goes over to non-serving team when balloon hits floor on serving team's side of net.

**Title:** BLOW BALL

**Number: 51**

**Goal:** Improve vital capacity.

**Objective:** Student will blow a ball 12 inches three out of five times.

**Environment:** Indoors or outdoors.

**Appropriate For:** Students with Muscular Dystrophy and limited vital capacity.

**Number of Players:** One to twelve.

**Equipment:** Ping-pong balls, chalk.

**Teaching Hints:**

1. Have students lie on carpet squares on their stomachs.
2. Use a straw to help blow the ball.
3. The student remains in the same spot.
4. Students should rest between blowing periods.

**Procedures:**

1. Set the ball on a line to begin the activity.
2. On the signal GO each student blows the ball as far as possible.
3. The score is the total number of inches the ball is blown.
4. The winner is the student with the highest score.

**Diagram**

**Students**

**Title:** WHEEL-A-ROUND

**Goal:** Improve mobility and endurance skills.

**Objective:** Students will maneuver, push and tag a student in another wheelchair.

| Environment: | Appropriate For: |
|---|---|
| Outdoors or indoors. | Wheelchairs only. |

| Number of Players: | Equipment: |
|---|---|
| Four to twelve. | None. |

**Teaching Hints:**

1. All students line up side by side twenty feet from the wheel-a-round circle.
2. Draw a circle for the wheel-a-round student.
3. After three or four turns, select a new Captain Wheeler.
4. Captain Wheeler starts the game by tagging the students.

**Procedures:**

1. Student sits in wheel-a-round circle and is called *Captain Wheeler*.
2. Other students slowly push their wheelchairs toward the wheel-a-round circle.
3. Students keep asking NOW-NOW and Captain Wheeler says NO-NO.
4. When Captain Wheeler says NOW all the students wheel-a-round and try to wheel back to the starting line.
5. Any of the students tagged help Captain Wheeler chase the students next time.

**Diagram**

Starting Line

Captain Wheeler

Wheel-a-Round Circle

**Title:** BEAN BAG BANDIT | **Number: 53**

**Goal:** Improve physical endurance skills.

**Objective:** Students will recover a bean bag and return it to home base in three out of five attempts.

**Environment:**

Outdoors.

**Appropriate For:**

All students.

**Number of Players:**

Six to thirty.

**Equipment:**

Cones, bean bags.

**Teaching Hints:**

1. Divide a large class into smaller groups.
2. Space the cones depending on the limitation of the students.
3. Allow a wheelchair student to have a pusher.

**Procedures:**

1. Designate a student as SHERIFF.
2. As the sheriff signals GO students walk, wheel, or run toward the bank. Each student attempts to steal one bean bag before the sheriff tags a bandit.
3. The tagged bandit becomes the sheriff and the game continues.

**Diagram**

**Title:** ALLIGATOR TAG | **Number: 54**

**Goal:** Increase upper motor strength.

**Objective:** Student will pull self and another student while on scooter board for a distance of 10 feet within 30 seconds.

**Environment:**
Indoors—smooth floor.

**Appropriate For:**
Elementary orthopedically handicapped.

**Number of Players:**
Six to twelve.

**Equipment:**
Scooter boards.

**Teaching Hints:**

**Procedures:**

1. Each player has own scooter board.
2. Two students are IT (or the alligator). The two students interlock feet while on the scooter boards. They then try to coordinate movement so as to tag another player. Either IT may tag another player. The player who is tagged then takes the place of the player who tagged him/her.
3. The alligators may lock feet in any way, but may not break the lock to tag another player.

| **Title:** PARACHUTE PLAY | **Number: 55** |
|---|---|

**Goal:** Increase arm and trunk strength.

**Objective:** Student will maintain straight arm reach overhead while holding parachute for 30 seconds.

| **Environment:** Outdoors or indoors. | **Appropriate For:** All students. |
|---|---|

| **Number of Players:** As many as can fit around parachute. | **Equipment:** One parachute. |
|---|---|

**Teaching Hints:**

1. Never bounce a student on top of the parachute.
2. Stress the fact that the whole class must work as a team.
3. Place adults around parachute as needed to help create a strong lift.

**Procedures:**

**Parachute basics:**

1. To get a good grip, have students roll the edge of the parachute towards the center, three or four times.
2. **Inflation:** On signal all students that can, squat and hold the parachute to the ground. On signal, everyone stretches arms up overhead. Try to get as much air as possible inside the chute. This is a basic stunt.
3. **Mushroom:** The Mushroom is made exactly like the Inflation. The air is sealed into the parachute by placing the edges of the parachute to the ground.

**Activities:**

1. Shake the parachute slowly making large waves.
2. Shake the parachute fast making small waves.
3. Pull the parachute tight and bounce a ball on the top of the parachute.
4. Let selected students run under the parachute while others hold tight.

**Movement Exploration Activities:**

1. Can you run with the parachute?
2. Can everyone do ten sit-ups holding on to the parachute?
3. Can you inflate the parachute and take three steps toward the middle?

**Title:** RED ROBIN

**Number: 56**

**Goal:** Improve running and mobility skills.

**Objective:** Student will walk, wheel, or run 15 yards in 20 seconds.

**Environment:**
Outdoors.

**Appropriate For:**
All students.

**Number of Players:**
Ten to thirty.

**Equipment:**
None.

**Teaching Hints:**
1. Allow wheelchair students to have a pusher if needed.
2. If a wheelchair student becomes the Red Robin, let him/her select a partner as a helper to tag other students.

**Procedures:**
1. Designate one student as the RED ROBIN.
2. Red Robin calls a player's name. The player runs or wheels toward the nest without being tagged. If the player is tagged, he/she becomes the Red Robin.
3. Two or more players' names can be called at the same time.
4. A player cannot be tagged in the nest area.

**Diagram**

61

**Title:** STEAL THE BACON     **Number: 57**

**Goal:** Improve physical endurance skills.

**Objective:** Student will wheel, walk or run to bean bag and pick it up on three out of five attempts.

| Environment: | Appropriate For: |
|---|---|
| Outdoors or indoors. | All students. |

| Number of Players: | Equipment: |
|---|---|
| Two to thirty. | Bean bags, chalk. |

**Teaching Hints:**

1. Vary the game by calling two numbers at a time.
2. For wheelchair students, elevate bean bag off ground. (Put bean bag on box, barrel or cone.)

**Procedures:**

1. Divide class into two teams with one team standing behind each goal line.
2. Players on each team can be in groups of four and numbered one to four.
3. When the teacher calls a number, the student with that number moves forward to try and pick up the bean bag and return across own goal line without being tagged by opponent.
4. Each player returning with the bean bag receives one point for his or her team.
5. The team with the most points wins the game.

| **Title:** STAR WARS | **Number: 58** |
|---|---|

**Goal:** Improve locomotion and physical fitness skills.

**Objective:** Students will run or move through a 25-yard star two out of five times in one minute.

**Environment:**

Outdoors.

**Appropriate For:**

Ambulatory students and students in wheelchairs.

**Number of Players:**

One to thirty.

**Equipment:**

Chalk, stopwatch, five cones.

**Teaching Hints:**

1. Draw star shape on cement or blacktop with chalk.
2. No more than four students should be placed on a team.
3. The points of the star are five yards apart.
4. Vary the size of the star according to the limitations of the students.

**Procedures:**

1. Divide class into equal number of teams.
2. On the signal GO each student starts on number one and runs or wheels to numbers two, three, four and five.
3. Each student's time is recorded.
4. The first team to complete the star gets a point.
5. The team with the most points wins the game.

**Diagram**

Finish

Start

**Title:** ALPHABET SWITCH

**Number: 59**

**Goal:** Improve endurance and mobility skills.

**Objective:** Student will move to another location before opposing team member in three out of five attempts.

**Environment:**

Outdoors or indoors.

**Appropriate For:**

Walkers and wheelchairs.

**Number of Players:**

Four to thirty.

**Equipment:**

Cones.

**Teaching Hints:**

1. Give each student a card with a letter on it.

**Procedures:**

1. Designate a student to be the leader.
2. Divide students into two teams facing each other.
3. The leader calls two letters such as A and D. All A's and D's move into the ''Ready'' area.
4. On the signal GO, A's and D's move around a cone and return to a new home.
5. The team which has everyone back first is the winner.

**Diagram**

Ready Area            Ready Area

B A                           A B

C D                           D C

B A                           A B

C D                           D C

Team A            Team B

**Title:** BASKETBALL HIGH POINT

**Number: 60**

**Goal:** Improve upper limb strength.

**Objective:** Student will throw a ball through a basketball hoop scoring two points in three out of five attempts.

**Environment:**

Indoors or outdoors.

**Appropriate For:**

Students with use of wrist, hand and shoulder.

**Number of Players:**

Two to five.

**Equipment:**

Low or high basket, any size ball.

**Teaching Hints:**

1. Vary the distance of the child to the basket depending on the ability of the child.
2. Attach basket to secure object so it does not fall over.
3. Place a barrel under the low basket to catch the balls.

**Procedures:**

1. Divide students into two teams.
2. Each student shoots the ball toward the basket or the barrel. The barrel is placed under the basket.
3. A basket shot counts two points and a barrel shot counts one point.
4. The team or student with the most points wins the game.

**Title:** TEN BASKETBALL

**Number: 61**

**Goal:** Improve arm strength.

**Objective:** Student will score ten baskets in five minutes.

**Environment:**
Outdoors.

**Appropriate For:**
Students with use of one arm.

**Number of Players:**
Two to six.

**Equipment:**
Basketballs, small balls, stopwatch, barrels (baskets).

**Teaching Hints:**

1. Draw a number grid on the blacktop with chalk.

2. Number the lines on the grid 1 through 10 with number 10 closest to the basket.

3. Have an aide stand at each basket to get the balls for the players.

**Procedures:**

1. Select two or more teams (two players on each team).

2. Each player stands or sits on line number one.

3. On the signal GO each player shoots at the basket.

4. After each successful shot, a player moves to the next highest number.

5. The winner is the player who reaches number ten first within a five-minute time period.

**Diagram**

| 10 |
| 9 |
| 8 |
| 7 |
| 6 |
| 5 |
| 4 |
| 3 |
| 2 |
| 1 |

Team A | Team B

**Title:** FOR SALE

**Number: 62**

**Goal:** Improve physical fitness.

**Objective:** Student will independently demonstrate three exercises on fitness card.

**Environment:**

Outdoors.

**Appropriate For:**

All students.

**Number of Players:**

Any number.

**Equipment:**

None.

**Teaching Hints:**

1. Teacher can use or modify any exercises appropriate for a particular group of students.

### Fitness Price Card

| | |
|---|---|
| 5 | Arm Circles |
| 10 | Finger Flicks |
| 5 | Jumping Jacks |
| 10 | Neck Circles |
| 5 | Waist Rotations |

**Procedures:**

1. Students form two teams facing each other approximately 20 yards apart.
2. One team is the BUYER team and the other team is the SELLER.
3. One team member of the seller team is chosen to be the THIEF.
4. At the teacher's signal all the buyers run to tag the sellers' baseline.
5. At the same time the thief must run and tag the opposite baseline.
6. As the thief returns to his own baseline, he/she must tag one buyer and take that person back to the seller's baseline.
7. After the price is set, all the buyers must perform the tasks in order to get back their own team member.
8. If the buyers perform and "pay the price" they are awarded back their team member.
9. The buyers now become the sellers and the sellers become the buyers. The process is repeated.

# Unit Three: Body Awareness

**Title:** SLOW RACING

**Goal:** Improve motor memory skills.

**Objective:** Student will, at the end of 30 seconds, be within five feet of the finish line in three out of five attempts.

| **Environment:** | **Appropriate For:** |
|---|---|
| Outdoors. | All students. |

| **Number of Players:** | **Equipment:** |
|---|---|
| Any number. | Stopwatch. |

**Teaching Hints:**

1. Teacher should stress safe and controlled walking with an awareness of self in relationship to other students or objects.

2. This game can be used effectively to *calm down* an active group before returning to the classroom.

**Procedures:**

1. Students line up on starting line.

2. Instructor demonstrates 30 seconds on stopwatch.

3. Students count out 30 seconds.

4. Students have 30 seconds to reach the twenty-foot finish line.

5. Anyone who reaches the finish line before the 30 seconds is disqualified.

6. Player on or nearest the finish line at the 30-second mark is the winner.

| Title: CREATIVE MOVEMENT OF PHYSICALLY HANDICAPPED | Number: 64 |
|---|---|

**Goal:** Increase creative movement abilities.

**Objective:** Student will demonstrate any type of movement to music for at least two minutes.

| Environment: | Appropriate For: |
|---|---|
| Indoors or outdoors. | All students. |

| Number of Players: | Equipment: |
|---|---|
| Any number. | Music. |

**Teaching Hints:**

Suggested material:

*The Art of Learning Through Movement* by Anne and Paul Barlin. Los Angeles: The Ward Ritchie Press.

*A Guide to Movement Exploration* by Layne C. Hackett and Robert G. Jenson. Palo Alto: Peek Publications.

*Movement Exploration and Games for the Mentally Retarded* by Layne C. Hackett. Palo Alto: Peek Publications.

**Procedures:**

Physically handicapped students can and do enjoy creative movement. Creative movement provides the teacher with an opportunity to discuss the differences and similarities of human movement. The student begins to understand that handicaps often require one to modify movement. However, students also learn that they can be creative and experience the joy of expressive movement.

**Suggested activities:**

1. Students move as certain music makes them "*feel.*"

2. Students imitate familiar objects of happenings. (*Examples:* An egg frying, a flower blooming, butter melting, different animals, etc.)

3. Students react with movement to a story read by the teacher.

**Title:** BODY ISOLATIONS

**Number: 65**

**Goal:** Improve body awareness.

**Objective:** Student will correctly identify by lifting three out of five basic body parts.

**Environment:**
Indoors or outdoors.

**Appropriate For:**
All students.

**Number of Players:**
Any number.

**Equipment:**
None.

**Teaching Hints:**

**Procedures:**

1. Start with head, trunk, hips, arms and legs. Have students shake, lift, or touch separate body parts, one at a time. Make sure students locate the correct body part.

2. Have students shake one part, continue shaking that part and add another. Continue to tolerance—do not allow students to become confused.

3. Repeat above procedure with more specific body parts.
   (*Example:* Eyes, nose, mouth, neck, shoulder, elbow, wrist, waist, knee and ankle.)

| **Title:** SHADOW TAG | **Number: 66** |
|---|---|

**Goal:** Increase body awareness, walking, and mobility skills.

**Objective:** Student will step into or on the shadow of another student within 30 seconds.

| **Environment:** | **Appropriate For:** |
|---|---|
| Outdoors—blacktop. | Walkers, wheelchair students. |

| **Number of Players:** | **Equipment:** |
|---|---|
| Two to twenty. | None. |

**Teaching Hints:**

1. Review body parts.
2. Plan to play the activity on a bright sunny day.
3. Use FREEZE as a signal for stop when the tempo of the activity intensifies.

**Procedures:**

1. Designate a student as IT.
2. IT tries to step or wheel onto another student's shadow.
3. IT tags the student, who becomes the new IT and the activity continues.
4. Each student gets a turn to be IT.

| **Title:** AIR MATTRESS ACTIVITY | **Number: 67** |
|---|---|

**Goal:** Improve balance.

**Objective:** Student will maintain knee standing posture while on inflated air mattress for 12 seconds.

**Environment:**
Indoors.

**Appropriate For:**
All students.

**Number of Players:**
One to six.

**Equipment:**
Air mattress.

**Teaching Hints:**

**Procedures:**

1. Students maintain balanced knee standing position while air mattress is inflated.
2. Students give thumbs up or thumbs down sign for the "*elevator*" to go up or down.
3. Students give imitation of animal movements while on air mattress. *Examples:* Bunny hop, snake crawl.
4. Students find own stripe and can not touch or roll into another stripe as the air mattress goes up and down.
5. Students have crawling, rolling, hopping and walking (supported by attending adult) relays.
6. Relaxation and maintaining position in space are emphasized, as mattress is inflated and deflated by teacher.

**Title:** PERFECT POSTURE RELAY | **Number: 68**

**Goal:** Improve standing and walking posture.

**Objective:** Student will walk or wheel self 10 feet without dropping bean bag off head.

**Environment:** Indoors or outdoors.

**Appropriate For:** All students.

**Number of Players:** Six to fourteen.

**Equipment:** Bean bag or wooden block.

**Teaching Hints:**

1. This game is very good for severely involved students who need to develop head control.

**Procedures:**

1. Students in wheelchairs play in chair.
2. Ambulatory students walk toe-heel manner.
3. Student places bean bag on head, walks or propels self to opposite line and returns. Student then gives bag to the next student in line.
4. If bag drops, student may stop and retrieve it, then continue.
5. No touching or holding the bag when moving.

**Title:** TOGETHERNESS (HIDE & SEEK)

**Goal:** Improve motor memory skills.

**Objective:** Student will, after locating IT, remember to hide and remain quiet for three minutes.

| **Environment:** | **Appropriate For:** |
|---|---|
| Outdoors. | All students. |

| **Number of Players:** | **Equipment:** |
|---|---|
| Any number up to 15. | None. |

**Teaching Hints:**

1. Have the last person who finds IT, be IT for the next game.

**Procedures:**

1. The person who is IT goes and hides.
2. All others in the group will turn their backs and count to a predetermined number, and **can not** look around to see where the person is hiding.
3. When number is reached, the group will spread out and search for the hidden person.
4. When one of the group finds the IT person, they will perform a brief exercise as determined by IT; e.g., arm circles, waist rotation, finger flicks, etc. They will then hide with IT and wait for more students.
5. The game is over when all students of the group find the IT person and are all hidden with that person.

**Title:** CRAYON DANCING

**Number: 70**

**Goal:** Improve body awareness.

**Objective:** Student will correctly identify head, shoulder, back, hips and feet.

**Environment:**
Indoors.

**Appropriate For:**
Students with use of hands.

**Number of Players:**
Any number.

**Equipment:**
Ten to twelve feet of butcher paper, crayons.

**Teaching Hints:**

1. Switch on Bach, John Denver, disco or any mood music.
2. Stress rhythm change and body awareness.

**Procedures:**

1. Tape butcher paper to hard floor. (Do not hand out crayons.)
2. Students should be out of chairs on the paper. Enlarge dimensions of paper if necessary.
3. Tell students that their head is a giant crayon, and that they should draw with their head exactly how the music makes them feel.
4. Play various types of rhythms of music. Point out the differences if students do not adjust to mood.
5. Repeat above procedure using shoulder, elbow, hand, buttocks, knees and feet.
6. Finally, give student a crayon and repeat process, drawing with crayon.

**Title:** BODY ISOLATION RELAYS

**Goal:** Increase body awareness and body/space relationships.

**Objective:** Student will correctly identify and lead with three out of four requested body parts.

**Environment:**

Indoor or outdoors.

**Appropriate For:**

All students.

**Number of Players:**

Any number.

**Equipment:**

None.

**Teaching Hints:**

1. For students who may need a particular body part for locomotion, exchange another part.

**Procedures:**

1. Have students form two or more teams.
2. Start relay by having students move to an *"end point"* leading with their head.
3. Second time through students lead with shoulders.
4. Repeat above procedures using elbow, hand, knees, buttocks and feet.
5. Relay may be broken into seven different relays or continued as one long relay.
6. First team to complete all seven races wins.

**Title:** WHISTLE STOP | **Number: 72**

**Goal:** Improve directionality and laterality.

**Objective:** Student will respond correctly to three out of four direction cues.

**Environment:**
Indoors or outdoors.

**Appropriate For:**
All students.

**Number of Players:**
Any number.

**Equipment:**
One whistle.

**Teaching Hints:**

1. Game can be made easier by always calling "forward" between other commands and waiting longer between commands.

2. Teacher may choose to have students point in requested direction first.

3. Game can be made more difficult by speeding up directions and starting off students facing different directions.

**Procedures:**

1. Students get in big circle facing the outside.

2. Teacher gives first direction of walking (or wheeling) straight.

3. At any given time the teacher blows the whistle and the students freeze in place.

4. The teacher then gives a new direction cue, waits five seconds and says GO.

5. Students then continue in that direction until whistle is again blown.

6. Procedure is repeated until "forward," "backward," "left," "right," "sideways," and "diagonal" are all called.

**Diagram**

**Title:** PRINGLE SOCCER

**Goal:** Improve upper body differentiation.

**Objective:** Student will hit a ball against a wall or with a partner at least 12 times in a row without losing possession of the ball.

**Environment:**
Indoors.

**Appropriate For:**
Students with use of arms.

**Number of Players:**
Six to fourteen.

**Equipment:**
Pringle cans or tennis balls cans, small rubber ball.

**Teaching Hints:**

1. Student may play using a wall as a "*partner*" in order to practice alone or keep the ball under greater control.

**Procedures:**

1. Students pair up and lay prone facing each other approximately 15 feet apart.

2. Each student has a Pringle can.

3. Student holds own Pringle can with two hands, arms extended.

4. Each pair tries to hit ball back and forth as many times as possible without hitting ball out of reach.

5. Total number of consecutive hits is figured for a designated length of time. Pair with highest total wins.

**Diagram**

**Title:** BODY PARTS MINI-GOLF

**Number: 74**

**Goal:** Increase body awareness and body/space relationships.

**Objective:** Student will hit target using requested body part three out of five attempts.

| Environment: | Appropriate For: |
|---|---|
| Indoors and outdoors. | All students. |

| Number of Players: | Equipment: |
|---|---|
| Any number. | Plastic golf ball for each player, chalk. |

**Teaching Hints:**

1. The game may be played on hands and knees.
2. The game may be played in crawling position using head or noses for the severely involved student.
3. The teacher may choose to change the body part used for each hole, or continue with the same body part throughout the entire course.

**Procedures:**

1. All students are given one plastic golf ball.
2. A mini-golf course is set up in playing area using chalk to draw the "*holes*."
3. There is no limit to the number of "*holes*" used.
4. The teacher will select which body part the student will use and refers to it as the "*putter*."
5. Each student takes turns playing one stroke at a time.
6. Each student keeps track of his or her own stroke total. Student with the lowest total wins.

**Title:** PARTNER PATTERNS

**Goal:** Improve body awareness.

**Objective:** Students will correctly mirror nine out of ten patterns presented by partner.

**Environment:**

Indoors and outdoors.

**Appropriate For:**

All students.

**Number of Players:**

Any even number.

**Equipment:**

None.

**Teaching Hints:**

1. Students can act out a particular animal or role (charade style).

2. Follower must mirror and attempt to guess the role or animal.

3. Stress that the leader is not trying to make the follower "*lose.*" The object is for the team to stay together.

**Procedures:**

1. All students choose a partner. (Students in wheelchairs should have their partner sit down at about eye level.)

2. One partner is chosen as the leader and the other is the follower.

3. The leader starts off by moving arms, head, neck, etc. in a variety of motions using a slow and deliberate movement.

4. The follower attempts to "*mirror*" the leader throughout the exercise.

5. At teacher cue, students change roles and repeat procedure.

# Unit Four: Social Behavior

**Title:** WET HEAD

**Number: 76**

**Goal:** Improve throwing accuracy.

**Objective:** Student will throw three out of four sponges through hole from a distance of four feet.

**Environment:**
Outdoor grassy area.

**Appropriate For:**
All students.

**Number of Players:**
Three to five per backboard.

**Equipment:**
Six small sponges, bucket, backboard with head hole, chair.

**Teaching Hints:**

1. Game can last for any determined time, depending on number of students, attempts desired for each student, and the time available.
2. Make sure sponges are small (2" x 2") or they may hurt.

**Procedures:**

1. Have volunteer sit behind backboard with head sticking through hole. Backboard may be painted with figure of clown or any other figure.
2. Students have six tries to hit the volunteer to make him a "*wet head.*"
3. Each hit is worth two points.
4. Student with most points wins a "*wet head is dead*" ribbon.

**Title:** IN AND OUT | **Number: 77**

**Goal:** Increase wheelchair mobility and hand-eye coordination skills.

**Objective:** Student will complete designed pattern course catching three out of five balls within 30 seconds.

**Environment:**

Outdoors.

**Appropriate For:**

Students in wheelchairs.

**Number of Players:**

Two.

**Equipment:**

Balls.

**Teaching Hints:**

1. Practice the wheeling patterns ahead of time.
2. Chalk the pattern on the cement or blacktop.

**Procedures:**

1. Assign player A or B to wheel an "*in*" or "*out*" pattern (see Diagram).
2. On the signal GO both players wheel their designated patterns.
3. The first player to his/her spot will get to have the ball thrown to them.
4. The winner will be the player who receives the most completed catches.

**Diagram**

Out    In        In    Out

Student A        Student B

**Title:** TEAM PASS THROUGH

**Number: 78**

**Goal:** Increase wheelchair mobility skills.

**Objective:** Student will pass through the obstacles in wheelchair within 30 seconds.

**Environment:**
Outdoors.

**Appropriate For:**
Students in wheelchairs.

**Number of Players:**
Two to twelve.

**Equipment:**
12 cones and stopwatch.

**Teaching Hints:**
1. Determine a boundary at the beginning of the activity.
2. Set up the obstacles (cones) in any varied fashion.

**Procedures:**
1. Divide the students into two equal teams.
2. Each team lines up on respective sides.
3. On the signal GO each team begins moving.
4. The team which goes through all the obstacles first and reaches the opposite end line wins the round.
5. Each round scores one point.
6. The team which scores the most points wins the game.

**Diagram**

Start                    Finish

A A A A A A    O  O  O  O  O  O

B B B B B B    O  O  O  O  O  O

**Title:** TURTLE POINTS

**Number: 79**

**Goal:** Improve wheelchair mobility and team co-operation.

**Objective:** Student will push wheelchair 15 feet in two out of four times in five minutes.

| **Environment:** | **Appropriate For:** |
|---|---|
| Outdoors or indoors. | Students in wheelchairs and walkers. |

| **Number of Players:** | **Equipment:** |
|---|---|
| One to twelve. | Stopwatch. |

**Teaching Hints:**

1. Mark off a distance of fifteen feet.
2. Emphasize that this activity is not a race.
3. Any number of students can comprise a "*turtle team.*" One student can be a "*turtle team.*"

**Procedures:**

1. Divide students into turtle teams.
2. The students with the "*slowest*" times score individual points for their respective team.
3. Each student attempts to travel fifteen feet in the slowest manner possible.
4. The student(s) with the lowest "*turtle points*" is the winner.

**Title:** TEAM PITCHBACK

**Goal:** Improve hand-eye coordination skills.

**Objective:** Student will catch two to five rebounds off the pitchback.

**Environment:**

Indoors or outdoors.

**Appropriate For:**

Walkers and wheelchair participants.

**Number of Players:**

Two to twenty.

**Equipment:**

Two pitchbacks, bean bags and yarn balls.

**Teaching Hints:**

1. An adult aide, or student aide, will need to hold the pitchbacks.

2. If the teams are large, the person holding the pitchback will have to rotate in line with the pitcher so all the children will be able to participate.

3. Discuss the definition of a catch (with the students) for scoring purposes.

**Procedures:**

1. Select two children to be CAPTAINS. The Captains pick teams of equal size.

2. Each team selects one child to be the pitcher. The pitcher stands behind the team members who are positioned in a semicircle facing the pitchback.

3. On the signal GO the pitcher throws the ball at the pitchback and a point is scored for the team that catches the ball.

4. The first team which successfully catches ten balls is the winner.

**Title:** BOMBARDMENT

**Number: 81**

**Goal:** Improve mobility, coordination and agility skills.

**Objective:** Students will improve throwing, catching and dodging skills on three out of five attempts in one minute.

**Environment:**
Outdoors or gymnasium.

**Appropriate For:**
Walkers and wheelchairs.

**Number of Players:**
Any number.

**Equipment:** Elementary blocks, Indian clubs, bowling pins, one or two balls, stopwatch.

**Teaching Hints:**

1. Play for 60-second periods. The winner would be the one who knocks down the most pins, blocks, or clubs in that time period.

2. Children with wheelchairs can block their pins, blocks or clubs.

3. Station helpers behind the blocks, pins or clubs to retrieve the balls.

**Procedures:**

1. Divide players into two teams.

2. Each team member can move around freely in their own area.

3. On signal GO, team A tries to hit and knock down opponent's blocks, clubs, or pins.

4. Team B keeps the pin, block, or clubs from being hit by the ball.

5. The team that knocks down all the pins or other objects is the winner.

**Diagram**

Helpers

Block
Pin
Club

Helpers

**Title:**   WATER BALLOON TOSS

**Goal:**   Improve throwing skills.

**Objective:**   Student will catch six-inch water balloon from five feet, four out of five attempts.

**Environment:**

Outdoors.

**Appropriate For:**

All students.

**Number of Players:**

Two to twenty.

**Equipment:**

Balloons filled with water.

**Teaching Hints:**

1. Fill the balloons with a small amount of water and blow up larger with air.

**Procedures:**

1. Divide students into partner groups.

2. Start with students facing one another about three feet apart.

3. Students both toss and catch balloon to one another at each one-foot mark.

4. Students continue to move backwards, catching and tossing the balloon on each successful catch until balloon is finally dropped or bursts.

5. Team throwing and successfully catching balloon from farthest distance wins.

**Diagram**

**Title:** NEWSPAPER BATTLES | **Number: 83**

**Goal:** Improve fine motor control.

**Objective:** Student will crush, with two hands, five double-page newspapers within thirty seconds.

**Environment:**
Indoor or outdoor—small area.

**Appropriate For:**
All students.

**Number of Players:**
Any number.

**Equipment:**
Eight-inch stack of newspapers, net, two barrels.

**Teaching Hints:**
1. Beware of newspaper print rubbing off on good clothing.

**Procedures:**

Divide class and newspapers into two teams. The teams will compete in four "*battles*" for one point each. Team with the most points after the four battles wins.

**Battles:**

1. Crumple up the stack of newspaper, one double page at a time. First team to finish up their stack wins.

2. Bomb other teams with crumpled newspaper for two minutes. After two minutes, call TIME and determine which team has most paper on their side.

3. Hide a body under a stack of newspaper. Team may choose any team member to hide. After three minutes of work time, teacher judges which team did the better job of hiding their body.

4. Each team forms a chain with a leader at the head beside the barrel. Newspaper stack is placed beside first person who picks up one piece at a time and passes the newspaper ball until it reaches the leader. The leader stuffs the ball into the barrel. The first team to stuff all the newspaper, with no pieces left on the ground, is the winner.

| **Title:** STING | **Number: 84** |
|---|---|

**Goal:** Improve individual mobility and ball handling skills.

**Objective:** Students will throw and bounce a ball at a moving target and hit the object four out of five times.

| **Environment:** | **Appropriate For:** |
|---|---|
| Outdoors. | Ambulatory and wheelchair students. |

| **Number of Players:** | **Equipment:** |
|---|---|
| Six to thirty-six. | Balls that bounce. |

**Teaching Hints:**

1. Emphasize team work between A and B to "*sting*" student C.
2. Position helpers or aides around the games to retrieve the balls.

**Procedures:**

1. Divide students into partner teams (three to a team).
2. Students A and B stand or sit fifteen or more feet apart.
3. Students A and B bounce the ball toward student C. If A or B bounces the ball past C to their partner and yells STING, A or B can throw the ball directly at C.
4. C must stay in the grid. If C is hit by the ball, the person bouncing the ball replaces C.

**Title:** COPY OR CHEAT

**Number: 85**

**Goal:** Improve visual motor memory.

**Objective:** Students will identify and perform six out of ten motor patterns in correct sequence.

**Environment:**
Indoors or outdoors.

**Appropriate For:**
All students.

**Number of Players:**
Any number.

**Equipment:**
None.

**Teaching Hints:**

1. The motions can be limited or modified sufficiently to include players in wheelchairs and other limitations.
2. Severely involved students may answer YES or NO as instructor repeats the pattern motions.

**Procedures:**

1. Players form circle and one player is chosen to start the game.
2. The first player makes a motion. The second player repeats that motion and adds one of his own. The player next to him repeats the first two motions, then adds his/her own, and so forth, around the circle.
3. If a player forgets one of the motions he may "*cheat*" and fake a motion in place of the original motion. If he/she is caught "*cheating*" or is unable to think of an additional motion of his/her own within 15 seconds, he/she then becomes the starter and the other players follow his/her motion and add their own.

**Title:** DONKEY TAG

**Goal:** Improve perceptual motor skills.

**Objective:** Student will maintain contact with partner for at least 30 seconds.

**Environment:**

Indoors or outdoors.

**Appropriate For:**

All students.

**Number of Players:**

Any number.

**Equipment:**

One rag per two students.

**Teaching Hints:**

**Procedures:**

1. Students pair up and contact each other in any manner, e.g., hands of one partner are placed on hips of other partner, or hands on handles of wheelchair, and so on.

2. The lead person becomes the donkey HEAD and the rear person becomes the TAIL.

3. The TAIL places a rag into a back pocket or ties it loosely to the back of wheelchair or walker.

4. All donkeys circulate trying to protect their rag, at the same time trying to grab other donkeys' rags.

5. Only the donkey HEAD may grab a rag.

6. As donkeys lose their rags they are out.

7. The last donkey to keep his or her rag is the winner.

**Title:** WHEELCHAIR TIC-TAC-TOE

**Number: 87**

**Goal:** Improve directionality and laterality.

**Objective:** Student will correctly identify "*three in a row*" in at least two different directions within 30 seconds.

**Environment:**

Outdoors or indoors— large area.

**Appropriate For:**

All students.

**Number of Players:**

Eight per tic-tac-toe square.

**Equipment:**

Chalk or masking tape.

**Teaching Hints:**

1. Make tic-tac-toe board as large as necessary to accommodate wheelchairs or walkers.

**Procedures:**

1. Draw a tic-tac-toe board with chalk or masking tape on blacktop approximately 9' x 9' square.

2. Divide students in two teams, one team being the X's and the other being the O's.

3. The first team sends one student out to any square of his or her choice. That student remains in that square.

4. The other team then sends out one student to any square that is not already taken.

5. The process continues until a team has three team members in a row.

6. Games with no winner (*cat's game*) are counted as ties.

7. One point is awarded for each win and the team with the most points after a given period of time is the winner.

**Diagram**

9'

9'

**Title:** CAPTURE THE BALL

**Number: 88**

**Goal:** Increase socialization and wheelchair mobility skills.

**Objective:** Student will capture the opponent's ball and return to own play area without being tagged.

**Environment:**

Outdoors—blacktop area.

**Appropriate For:**

Walkers, students with wheelchair mobility.

**Number of Players:**

Six to ten.

**Equipment:**

Two cones, two tennis balls.

**Procedures:**

1. Divide students into two teams.

2. Each team tries to steal or capture the other team's ball. If the ball is returned over the division line, the team capturing the ball scores a point.

3. If a player is tagged in the opposing team area, they go to the opposing team's penalty box.

4. Team members held in the penalty box can only leave when they are released or tagged by a member of their own team. The team member returning from the penalty box gets a free wheel/walk back to their own side.

**Teaching Hints:**

1. Use any variation appropriate for students.

2. Allow for strategy amongst team members.

3. Students can "*huddle*" together to plan an attack on opposing team.

4. Select a Team Captain and let them make decisions regarding the course of the game.

**Diagram**

99

# Unit Five: Recreation

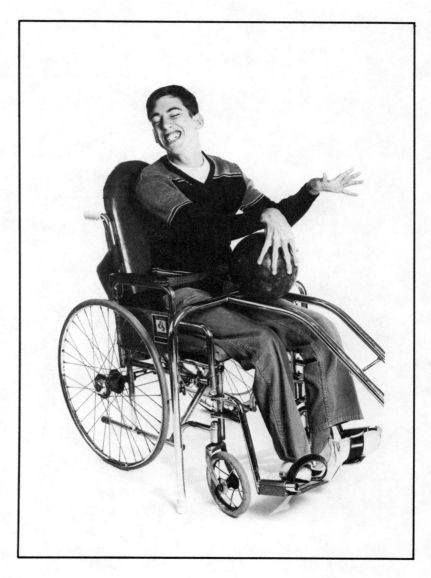

**Title:** SHUFFLEBOARD PUSH

**Goal:** Increase pushing skills.

**Objective:** Student will push shuffleboard disc onto grid in three out of five attempts.

**Environment:**
Indoors or outdoors.

**Appropriate For:**
Students with mild handi- capping conditions.

**Number of Players:**
Two to four.

**Equipment:**
Four discs, four pushing sticks.

**Teaching Hints:**

1. Emphasize pushing the disc slowly.
2. Modify the distance of the dead space according to the limitations of the students.
3. Set up grid on a table—students can push disc with their hand.
4. For advanced players, increase each number by adding a zero to the existing number.
5. Colors and letters can be used in place of numbers.

**Procedures:**

1. Students push discs from their own starting line. (Use stick or push with hand.)
2. The disc must land inside opponent's triangle to score.
3. Points do not count if the disc lands on a line.
4. A student can have an assist by moving up to the dead line if necessary.
5. The student with the highest score is the winner.

**Diagram**

Starting Line    Dead Lines    Starting Line

**Title:** FENCE BASKETBALL

**Number: 90**

**Goal:** Improve and maintain shoulder strength.

**Objective:** Student will score three baskets from the key within three minutes.

**Environment:**
Outdoors.

**Appropriate For:**
All students.

**Number of Players:**
Six to ten.

**Equipment:**
Basketball hoop, backboard with hooks on back, basketball.

**Teaching Hints:**
1. Use this game as a lead up to basketball.
2. Stress guarding and shooting skills.
3. More skills can be incorporated as skill level increases.

**Procedures:**
1. Students form two teams.
2. Game starts from back court line. Coin toss determines which team starts with the ball.
3. One player from each team approaches hoop. Player with the ball dribbles (or carries ball in lap, etc.) while the other player guards him or her.
4. Once the two players reach the key (determined by skill level of players), the player with the ball receives three free throws. If player makes any of the free throws, he or she is awarded one more shot.
5. The ball is then turned over to the other player who takes three free throws.
6. The two players return to the back court and pass the ball to the next two players.
7. Score is totaled for all players. Team with most points wins.
8. One basket equals one point.

**Title:** FOUR SQUARE

**Goal:** Improve hand-eye coordination.

**Objective:** Students will make contact with ball in three out of five attempts.

**Environment:**
Outdoors, four squares; each square 5' x 5'.

**Appropriate For:**
Ambulatory students and students with upper body mobility.

**Number of Players:**
Four.

**Equipment:**
Large rubber ball or beach ball.

**Teaching Hints:**
1. Number squares with chalk one to four.
2. Allow four students per game.
3. Allow wheelchair students to place wheels outside of square (shown on diagram).
4. Students in wheelchairs can hit the ball with one hand, two hands, or bat the ball with the fist.

**Procedures:**
1. One student stands or sits in each square.
2. The game starts when player number four bounces the ball to other players.
3. The ball must land in the opponent's square and be played after the first bounce.
4. The receiving player bounces it to another player.
5. The ball must be bounced once in a square before it can be returned to another player.
6. The ball cannot be held or caught.
7. The player that fouls goes to square one. Other players move in regular rotation from 1 to 2 to 3 to 4.
8. Other rules can be made up before game starts.

**Diagram**

Wheelchair Circle

105

| **Title:** KICKBALL | **Number: 92** |
|---|---|

**Goal:** Improve foot-eye coordination and endurance.

**Objective:** Student will kick ball a distance of ten feet.

| **Environment:** Outdoors, blacktop surface. | **Appropriate For:** All students. |
|---|---|

| **Number of Players:** Six to twelve. | **Equipment:** Soccerball or cageball (small), four bases. |
|---|---|

**Teaching Hints:**

1. A child in a wheelchair can throw the ball.
2. A walker with crutches can hit the ball with his or her crutch.
3. A substitute kicker may also be provided for the student in a wheelchair.

**Procedures:**

1. Divide the players into two teams.
2. Pitcher rolls the ball to the kicker.
3. The pitcher throws the ball to a student in a wheelchair.
4. Each player who is "*up*" gets three rolls or three catches.
5. If the ball is not kicked or caught in three attempts, the student is "*out.*"

| **Title:** SOFTBALL | **Number: 93** |

**Goal:** Improve batting, fielding skills, pitching, throwing, catching and moving from base to base.

**Objective:** Students will independently demonstrate proper base sequence in three out of five attempts.

**Environment:**
Outdoors, softball diamond (blacktop).

**Appropriate For:**
Students in wheelchairs, walkers.

**Number of Players:**
Ten to twenty.

**Equipment:**
Softball and bat, three bases, home plate, catcher's mask.

**Teaching Hints:**

1. Using a batting-T if needed.
2. Use a plastic bat if regular is too heavy.
3. Use a six-inch playground ball and let the ball take one bounce between the pitcher and the batter.
4. Vary the distance of the bases according to the ability of the students.
5. Wheelchair students can have pushers if needed.
6. The circles in diagram are ''safe areas'' for wheelchairs.

**Procedures:**

1. Bat the ball into the fair zone and walk, wheel or run to first base.
2. Continue to walk, wheel, or run to second and third base if it is safe.
3. The batting team remains at bat until three outs are made.
4. After three outs, teams exchange sides.
5. A turn at bat for each team completes an inning.

**Diagram**

**107**

**Title:** GUTS FRISBEE

**Number: 94**

**Goal:** Improve catching and throwing skills.

**Objective:** Student will catch five out of ten frisbees thrown from a distance of ten feet.

**Environment:**

Outdoors or gymnasium.

**Appropriate For:**

Students with some use of wrist and hand.

**Number of Players:**

Eight or ten on each team.

**Equipment:**

One frisbee.

**Procedures:**

1. Form two lines about 20 feet apart, facing each other, out-stretched arms, fingertip to fingertip. (May be adjusted to abilities of students.)
2. Players flip frisbee back and forth between teams.
3. The frisbee must not be out of reach of other players.
4. If the frisbee is out of reach of a team, then that team gets a point.
5. If the frisbee is within reach and is missed, then the throwing team gets a point.

**Teaching Hints:**

1. Try to place students with equal abilities across from each other.
2. Caution students about throwing too hard.
3. Nerf frisbees work very well for students with limited skill.

**Diagram**

**Title:** LAP SHUFFLE BALL

**Goal:** Improve perceptual motor skills.

**Objective:** Student will score a total of at least 20 points in five shots.

**Environment:**
Indoors and outdoors.

**Appropriate For:**
Students with some arm use.

**Number of Players:**
Two to four.

**Equipment:**
Small rubber ball and lap shuffleboard.

**Teaching Hints:**

1. A lap shuffleboard can easily be made from plywood or stiff cardboard.

**Procedures:**

1. Each student is given five shots. Each hole on shuffleboard is marked with a point value. Student tries to accumulate highest total points.

2. Turns are rotated and/or repeated, depending on time allowances.

**Diagram**

**Title:** FRISBEE GOLF

**Goal:** Improve perceptual motor skills.

**Objective:** Students will contact cone with a frisbee from a distance of 10 feet two out of three times.

**Environment:**
Outdoors, grass or hardtop area.

**Appropriate For:**
Students with arm use.

**Number of Players:**
Four to ten.

**Equipment:**
Frisbees (ring, bean bags, nerf balls may also be used).

**Teaching Hints:**

**Procedures:**

1. Cones are patterned on grass or hardtop area approximately 15 feet apart.

2. Players take turns attempting to hit cones with frisbee.

3. Players leave frisbees where it lands each turn. Player then throws it from that spot for the next turn.

4. Players may not proceed unless cones are hit in successive order.

5. Lowest total number of throws per course determines winner.

**Diagram**

**Title:** RAMP BOWLING

**Goal:** Improve perceptual motor skills.

**Objective:** Student will knock down six out of 10 bowling pins in two rolls.

| **Environment:** | **Appropriate For:** |
|---|---|
| Outdoors. | All students. |

| **Number of Players:** | **Equipment:** |
|---|---|
| Four per ramp. | Bowling ramp, bowling ball, ten bowling pins. |

**Teaching Hints:**

Bowling ramps can be ordered from:

Roll-a-Ball Ramp
Ms. Margaret Lee
Highway 18 East
Mason City, Iowa 50401

**Procedures:**

1. Set up regular ten-pin bowling cluster approximately 30 feet from end of ramp.
2. Each player has two rolls to knock down as many pins as possible.
3. Score is kept on large chalk board in traditional bowling style.

**Variation—Indian Bowling**

Set up cluster of three Indian clubs on a one-foot triangle for each team, if more than one team is involved.

Team is lined up 20 feet from pins, or distance appropriate to skill level. First player rolls his ball, and he continues rolling the ball until all pins are down. The pinsetter returns ball until all pins are down. Then player number two begins.

1. On the signal GO the players push or roll the ball. The player that makes the ball roll across the table and onto the barrel first, scores one point. If the ball is thrown into the barrel, the player scores a bonus point.
2. The winner is the player with the most points.

**Title:** BASKET BARREL | **Number: 98**

**Goal:** Improve or maintain arm and shoulder strength.

**Objective:** Score a basket on three out of five attempts.

**Environment:**
Indoors or outdoors.

**Appropriate For:**
Students with very little upper body strength and mobility.

**Number of Players:**
Two to four.

**Equipment:**
Long table (two players), two barrels, two balls.

**Teaching Hints:**
1. Position players on the same side of a long table.
2. Place a basket (barrel) opposite each student, next to the table.

**Procedures:**
1. On the signal GO the players push or roll the ball. The player that makes the ball roll across the table and into the barrel first scores one point. If the ball is thrown into the barrel, the player scores a bonus point.
2. The winner is the player with the most points.

**Diagram**

**Title:** WHEELCHAIR JAZZ-EX

**Goal:** Improve gross motor fitness.

**Objective:** Student will independently perform one jazz exercise routine for two minutes.

**Environment:**
Indoors.

**Appropriate For:**
Students with upper motor control.

**Number of Players:**
Any number.

**Equipment:**
Popular records, record player.

**Teaching Hints:**

**Procedures:**

The following examples of jazz exercise routines can be adapted for most ability levels. These routines were designed for wheelchair students. Ambulatory students can perform them standing or sitting in a chair. In all cases the beat is the important factor. Any music with a good fast beat can be used.

Suggested music—"*Rock With You*" by Michael Jackson.

**Exercises:**

1. Arm circles, eight counts forward—eight counts backward.
2. Knees open and close for sixteen counts.
3. Boxing (closed fists punching straight out in front) for sixteen counts.
4. Swim backstroke for sixteen counts.
5. Swim crawlstroke for sixteen counts.
6. Finger flicks for sixteen counts.

Repeat.

| | |
|---|---|
| **Title:** WHEELCHAIR TOUCH FOOTBALL | **Number: 100** |

**Goal:** Increase gross motor skills.

**Objective:** Students will catch three out of five thrown nerf footballs from a distance of five feet.

| **Environment:** Outdoor—blacktop area. | **Appropriate For:** All students. |
|---|---|

| **Number of Players:** Sixteen. | **Equipment:** Nerf football, six cones, stopwatch or clock. |
|---|---|

**Teaching Hints:**

1. Stress safety and blocking methods which avoid contact.
2. Combine wheelchair football with a spectator skill unit and/or field trip to a high school football game.

**Procedures:**

1. Each half shall be 25 minutes. Each team is allowed two time-outs each half.
2. There shall be a ten-minute half-time.
3. In order to receive a first down, midfield must be crossed.
4. The teams shall consist of eight players: five players on the line and three backs.
5. There will be kick off; ball will be put in play on the 20-yard line.
6. No blocking for the ball carrier on punts.
7. The offensive line must wait to cover punts until the ball has been kicked or thrown.
8. Line player can not advance a fumble recovery.
9. Wheelchair pushers may use bridal step only.
10. A nerf football will be used.
11. The team coach may receive passes intended for receivers unable to catch.

**Penalties:**

- Illegal use of hands.
- Flagrant offsides.
- Locking other wheelchair brakes.
- Bumping into body, walker, or wheelchair.

**Title:** PIN BOWLING

**Goal:** Improve hand-eye coordination skills.

**Objective:** Student will release the ball with two hands and knock down three pins in one minute.

**Environment:**
Outdoors.

**Appropriate For:**
Students with upper body mobility.

**Number of Players:**
One or two.

**Equipment:**
Swinging tetherball, bowling pins or blocks.

**Teaching Hints:**
1. Suspend rope of tetherball from screw eye overhead.
2. Ask a student or aide to help set up pins and to keep score.
3. Position the wheelchair so the ball will not hit the student sitting in the wheelchair.
4. Draw small circles on cement to position pins.
5. Position pins on chalk marks previously drawn on cement.
6. Vary the challenge of the activity by spacing pins farther apart.

**Procedures:**
1. Each player has one minute to knock down three or more pins. On the signal GO player A releases the ball toward the pins.
2. At the end of one minute, player B releases the ball at the pins.
3. The winner is the player which knocks down the greatest number of pins in one minute.

**Diagram**

**DATE DUE**

|  |  |  |  |
|---|---|---|---|
|  |  |  |  |
|  |  |  |  |
|  |  |  |  |
|  |  |  |  |
|  |  |  |  |
|  |  |  |  |
|  |  |  |  |
|  |  |  |  |
|  |  |  |  |
|  |  |  |  |
|  |  |  |  |
|  |  |  |  |